COMMITTED
TO BUDDHISM

A BUDDHIST COMMUNITY

SYLVIA AND BARRY
SUTCLIFFE

RMEP

RELIGIOUS AND MORAL EDUCATION PRESS

Religious and Moral Education Press
An imprint of Chansitor Publications Ltd,
a wholly owned subsidary of Hymns Ancient & Modern Ltd
St Mary's Works, St Mary's Plain
Norwich, Norfolk NR3 3BH

First published 1995

ISBN 1-85175-030-4

Acknowledgements
The Authors and Publisher would like to thank the
sangha at Amaravati Buddhist Monastery, including members of
the lay community, for their help and cooperation in preparing
this book. We are especially indebted to the people who gave up
their time to be interviewed and to Amaro Bhikku for being our
principal contact.

The photograph on page 33, by Susan and Alan Parker,
is reproduced by permission of Planet Earth Pictures.

Designed and typeset by Topics Visual Information, Exeter

Photography by Michael Burton-Pye

Printed in Singapore by Tien Wah Press for
Chansitor Publications Ltd, Norwich

CONTENTS

INTRODUCTION

The books in this **Faith and Commitment** series give you the chance to look at religions and religious denominations (groups within religions) through the personal reflections of people with a religious commitment.

To create these books, we visited local religious communities in different parts of Britain. We talked to people across the range of ages and roles you'd expect to find in a community – parent, child, grandparent, priest, community worker. That is, we interviewed people like you and your family, your friends, the people where you live. We asked them all the same questions and we've used the themes of those questions as chapter headings in the books.

Each chapter contains extracts from those interviews. People interpret our questions as they want to. They talk freely in their own words about religious ideas and personal experiences, putting emphasis where they think it belongs for them. The result is a set of very individual insights into what religion means to some of the people who practise it. A lot of the insights are spiritual ones, so you may have had similar thoughts and experiences yourself, whether or not you consider yourself a 'religious' person.

You will see that some pages include FACT-FINDER boxes. These are linked to what people say in the interview extracts on these pages. They give you bits of back-up information, such as a definition or where to look up a reference to a prayer or a piece of scripture. Remember that these books are not textbooks. We expect you to do some research of your own when you need to. There are plenty of sources to go to and your teacher will be able to help.

There are also photographs all through the books. Some of the items you can see belong to the people whose interview extracts appear on those pages. Most of these items have personal significance. Some have religious significance, too. They are very special to the people who lent them for particular but different reasons, like special things belonging to you.

Committed to Buddhism: A Buddhist Community introduces you to seven Buddhists who are either members of the sangha of monks and nuns at Amaravati Buddhist Monastery in Great Gaddesden or part of its lay community. 'Amaravati' means 'Deathless Realm' in Pali (see page 9), a reminder of where a Buddhist's spiritual journey is heading. The monastery is in the Theravada Buddhist tradition.

SYLVIA AND BARRY SUTCLIFFE

4

ABOUT ME

NAME: *Tissa F*

WHAT I DO: *I'm doing A-levels at the moment, in Psychology, Biology and German and A/S RE. I do the Psychology outside school.*

MY FAMILY: *I've got two sisters. One's older and one's a twin. My older sister's nineteen and at college in London doing Dance. My twin sister's doing A-levels like me, although she's more into Art. Her Buddhist name's Nimala, which means 'pure'.*

SOME OF MY SPECIAL INTERESTS: *I used to do a lot of judo. With my sister, I went in for a national kata competition. In kata you don't fight an opponent, you do set moves and sequences. We came fifth, which was quite good. But we don't have a lot of time now, so we've finished that, really. I also used to be in a brass band – I play trombone, my sister plays trumpet.*

MORE ABOUT ME

I've been called Tissa since I was six years old. When we were six, Mum asked us if we wanted Buddhist names. We didn't have to have one. Mum got her name at the same time as we got ours. There's no normal age when this happens. Some parents get names for their babies, some people get names for themselves as adults.

You request a Buddhist name from one of the monks. I got mine from Ajahn Sumedho, the Head Monk at Amaravati. The monk also gives you the Five Precepts. He chants them one by one and you repeat them. The Five Precepts are principles that were laid down by the Buddha. They're not rules or commandments, as such. They're ways of behaving that we agree to follow. We agree not to kill, steal, lie – things like that.

The reason I'm a vegetarian is because I've agreed not to kill. Everyone in our family's a vegetarian, apart from Dad. He likes his meat! We don't mind. What I can't stand is people who are vegetarian and preach it: 'Everyone else has got to be vegetarian.' I see it as quite natural for people to want to eat meat, but I don't want to eat it myself.

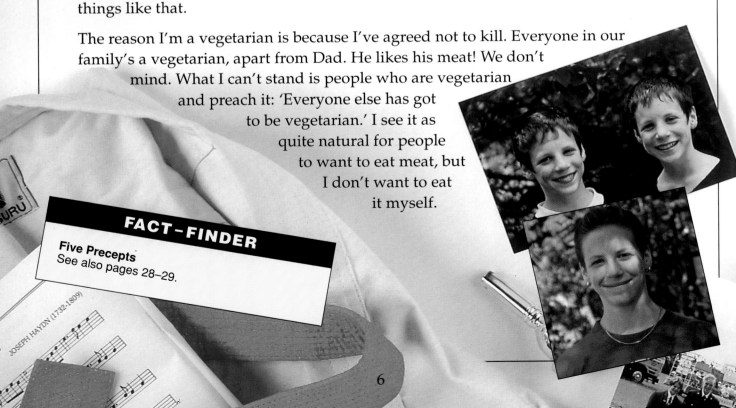

FACT–FINDER

Five Precepts
See also pages 28–29.

NAME:	*Medhina F. 'Medhina' is a Buddhist name meaning 'one is wise'.*
WHAT I DO:	*I'm forty-six years old. My main activities are education and Buddhism. I teach primary-age children. I've been teaching for about eighteen years.*
MY FAMILY:	*My dad was a Lancashire lad and my mum's Belgian. They met in the Second World War. I got married about twenty-five years ago and we have three girls.*
SOME OF MY SPECIAL INTERESTS:	*In the past, I used to have more wide-ranging interests — needlework, sport and things like that. But there isn't much time left between having a family of three children, a career and a big interest like Buddhism.*

MORE ABOUT ME

I started studying Buddhism, reflecting and meditating in an informal way on my own from about the age of fourteen. For many years, I was quite an isolated Buddhist. Then I decided I wanted to find out what other Buddhists looked like and joined the Buddhist Society in London. They put me in touch with the Theravada Buddhist monastery at Chithurst in Sussex, but I had to travel long distances to keep up the contact. Then a few years later this second Theravada monastery was opened at Amaravati. It's much nearer my home. Now I come here regularly.

I'm very grateful that we have this sangha here in England. At the beginning, I was practising Buddhism on my own, intellectually. That's a completely different thing to being with real people living out the Buddhist tradition in their daily lives. They're dealing with the human problems of living with each other in the twentieth century. They're also dealing with modern technology. Yet somehow they are still living a vinaya set down 2500 years ago. And it works, the system works! That is why Buddhism is alive for me, because it works in these people. It's the proof of the pudding.

FACT-FINDER

Sangha
Here, community of (Buddhist) monks and nuns.

Living a vinaya
Living according to rules of discipline for Buddhist monks/nuns.

NAME: *Jitindriya*

WHAT I DO: *I'm thirty-one years old. About five years ago I was ordained as a nun at Amaravati. That's when I was given my Pali name: Jitindriya. 'Jit' means 'victory over' and 'indriya' means 'the senses'. For two years before that, I was a novice.*

MY FAMILY: *I come from Australia. My mother was Roman Catholic, my father was agnostic. My mother brought us up as Catholics until we were old enough to decide for ourselves whether we would still go to church or not. Each of us decided not to. It didn't mean a lot to us then.*

SOME OF MY SPECIAL INTERESTS: *We live a renunciant life here — we give up, renounce, lots of things. Much of our time is spent in solitary meditation, prayer and personal reflection. Much of our contemplation is about the way our minds work and how our personalities are created. So my personal interests are really tied up with my spiritual practice.*

MORE ABOUT ME

I came to this monastery for the first time on a retreat. I was about twenty-three. I'd left Australia, travelled across South-East Asia and come to England. I'd being trying to put together my own little jigsaw of the world, trying to understand it. It was on that retreat that all the pieces of the puzzle came together. At last! Here was a 2500-year-old tradition able to give me the rest of the ideas I'd been looking for. It also offered me a practical way forward that I could take up and develop. I realized that my search had been a valid one.

It didn't even occur to me then that I'd put myself forward to be a nun. I remember thinking, looking at the monks and nuns, 'They're a community of special people, they're not me.' I thought, 'I've got to become special to be one of them.'

Every time I came back to Amaravati I understood a little bit more about the community and its structure. I realized that the monks and nuns were very ordinary people like me. Slowly it dawned on me that it would be possible for me to ordain if I wanted to. Because my priorities were changing, this became something I had to consider seriously. Within a year, I'd more or less decided to ordain. I think my heart clicked straight away, but it can take a long time for the rational mind to get there.

The first ordination ceremony for a Buddhist monk or nun is called the 'going forth'. Traditionally you reflect at this time on going forth from home into homelessness. In going forth, you give up not just the home comforts but what could be called the attachments that tie you to a specific family. They're not cut off – we don't discourage contact with families. But a Buddhist monk or nun has to go from the security of belonging to one particular family to becoming part of a larger family. I think of it as joining the family of humankind.

As a Buddhist nun, I've also given up anything to do with money. I have no means to support myself financially. I can't own property. All we nuns and monks have given to us and all we can consider our own are what we call the Four Requisites: alms-bowl, robes, medicine if we need it, and shelter for one night. Even when we're living in a monastery, we remember that all we're being offered is shelter for one night. The reflection is always: 'This isn't my place. This is shelter that's been offered to me.' So all the means we might have to support ourselves are removed. We can't even keep food overnight for our own personal use.

When Ajahn Chah, who founded our monastery, brought the first four Theravada Buddhist monks to Britain, he insisted that they should continue with the alms-round. In Thailand every morning at dawn, Buddhist monks go out with their alms-bowls and walk through the villages. People offer rice and other things to eat into the bowls. The monks then go back to the monastery and share out the food. That's their meal for the day.

In continuing the tradition here, we do go out with our alms-bowls. Sometimes we're invited to people's houses – friends of the community might ask us to visit them. When they bring us back to the monastery, they often offer food into our bowls. At other times, we go on an alms-round to the local village in faith that people might offer us something to sustain us for the day. Ample food is offered. It's quite surprising. People who don't know about our traditions sometimes offer money, but we can only accept food for our daily meal. We're not allowed to ask, we can only receive.

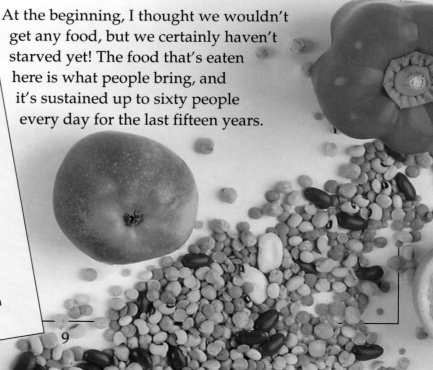

At the beginning, I thought we wouldn't get any food, but we certainly haven't starved yet! The food that's eaten here is what people bring, and it's sustained up to sixty people every day for the last fifteen years.

FACT-FINDER

Pali
Ancient Indian language in which the main Theravada Buddhist sacred books are written.

Ordained
Here, ordination is the Buddhist ceremony at which a person is ordained (made) a nun or monk.

Novice
Here, someone accepted into a Buddhist monastery in training before taking the full set of vows necessary to become a nun.

Agnostic
Someone who believes that humans cannot know (or find out) whether or not God exists.

Retreat
Going on a retreat means going somewhere away from the distractions of everyday life in order to meditate or reflect.

NAME: *Amaro*

WHAT I DO: *I'm Second Monk here at Amaravati. That means that when the Abbot, who's head of the community, is away or travelling, I help guide the community and am the front person for it.*

I'm English by birth. I've been a monk for fifteen years and have lived most of that time in this country, like many of the monks and nuns at Amaravati. I trained as a novice in Thailand for about two years, then returned to England shortly after the Theravada monastery at Chithurst in Sussex opened.

MY FAMILY

To me, becoming a Buddhist monk in Thailand was the natural extension of an interest in spirituality I'd had since childhood. My family was horrified. To them, it was throwing everything to the winds. They knew I was eccentric and rebellious, a person of extremes, but they'd never associated me with anything religious. What I'd done was something that just didn't have a place in their world. As far as they were concerned, after a couple of years of sowing wild oats I'd be coming back to settle down, get a haircut, get a job, get married. They were very kind, but they were bewildered.

Once I was back in England, my family could come to the monastery at Chithurst to visit me. It wasn't until then that they began to realize that, although it was all very peculiar, there was a wholesomeness to this Buddhist life. We were working hard to restore a dilapidated Victorian mansion. We were putting a lot of energy into the gardens. They couldn't understand it, but at least they could see it was harmless.

10

Parents need to be proud of their children. The heart searches for something to be glad about in the family. Several years later, I realized this. Long walks are traditional in our community. I did one of the first in this country in 1983, from the monastery in Sussex to the one in Northumberland. Afterwards I wrote a book about it which I dedicated to my parents. Up until then, I'd given them nothing to latch on to, nothing that they could talk to their friends about. Suddenly they were proud of me, and I saw how painful it must have been for them before.

As my parents have got older, I've also seen how what we call in Buddhism the Heavenly Messengers – old age, sickness, death – have become more prominent in their world. My father died last year, and during the last few years he naturally started to review his life and put it into context. I found this extraordinary. My father had been a very dynamic, busy person who travelled the world judging dog shows and wrote books about dogs. He was the most down-to-earth man imaginable. But seeing life drawing to a close, faced with questions like 'What was it all for?', he changed. He certainly seemed to develop, if not a religious sense, then certainly an awe at the laws and ways of nature. Both my parents did. I think it was partly due to having me around in the family: photographs of this shaven-headed character about the house. So, in the end, the effect of my life and choice hasn't been destructive to them. In a roundabout way, I feel it's given them a great spiritual resource.

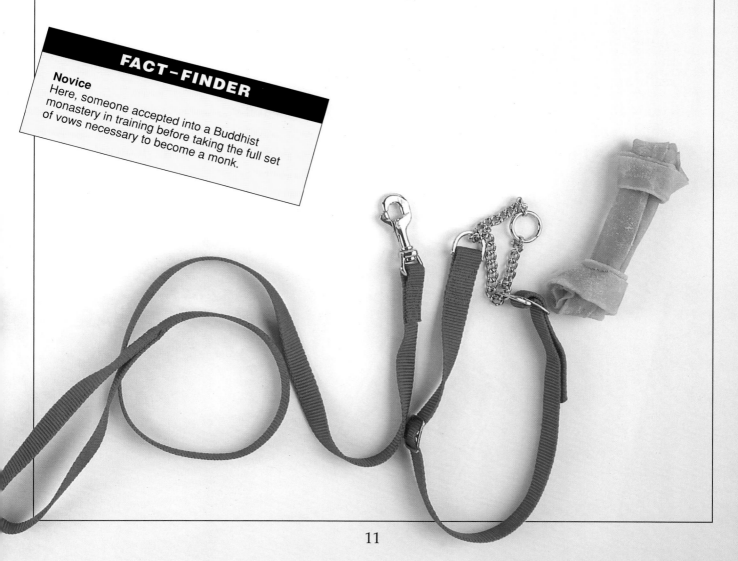

FACT-FINDER

Novice
Here, someone accepted into a Buddhist monastery in training before taking the full set of vows necessary to become a monk.

NAME: *Maurice*

WHAT I DO: *I'm a retired university teacher. I was always good at languages at school and taught German at London University.*

MY ROLE IN THE RELIGIOUS COMMUNITY

I'm keen to spread knowledge of Buddhism around because it's been very valuable to me and I believe it's a very valuable thing for the world. So I've tried to do my little bit: lecturing and teaching, that sort of thing. I'm not really a Buddhist scholar, but I like to call myself a scholarly Buddhist. I've no degrees in Sanskrit or anything of that kind, but my academic training and understanding have helped me get a good grasp of Sanskrit and Pali.

The earliest Buddhist scriptures, which are followed by Theravada Buddhism, are in Pali. It's an ancient Indian language which was obviously widespread in the Buddha's time, a kind of simplified Sanskrit. There are a lot of philosophical and other special words in the Pali language which you have to learn to understand. For Western scholars, that hasn't been easy.

The monks and the nuns at Amaravati chant in Pali and lay people try to pick up the shorter bits. I try to help them get it right – pronounce it right and understand what the words really mean. I'm looked up to as a bit more of an expert in this area than I really am, perhaps!

I don't live terribly far from Amaravati. I come over here at weekends, mainly. I've actually spent three months as a monk. My wife died in 1988. The following year I was invited to join the sangha here. They said that, in view of my long service and experience, I wouldn't have to go through the usual two years of devotion in white: I could come straight in.

Peace an...
Ajahn Sumedho
Ajahn Anando

The Way It...

Ajahn Sumedho

FACT-FINDER

Sanskrit
Ancient Indian language used in most Hindu and some (Mahayana) Buddhist sacred books.

Lay people
Here, Buddhists who are not monks or nuns.

Sangha
Here, community of (Buddhist) monks and nuns.

Devotion in white
'White' refers to the colour of the robes worn by a Buddhist novice. Someone who wants to be a monk usually first has to spend some time living in a monastery in training as a novice.

I felt that was the kind of offer I couldn't refuse. I said, 'Right, I'll stick it out for three months if it kills me.' And I did, and it didn't. I found it a marvellous experience, very beneficial in all sorts of ways. After the three months, I gave it up again and returned to lay life. That's quite a normal thing to do in Buddhism, especially in the Thai Theravada tradition.

NAME: *Ron*

WHAT I DO: *I'm forty-two years old and a novice here at Amaravati with the intention of being ordained a monk. I've been a novice for two months and have another two years to go.*

MY FAMILY: *I have as close as you can probably get to a normal background. I come from an average sort of family, had a pretty average sort of education at school, did a degree in chemistry then worked as an Environmental Health Officer.*

My parents were nominally Church of England but not particularly religious. We'd go to church when there were births, deaths or marriages in the family. I went to Sunday school now and then.

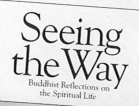

FACT-FINDER

Novice • Ordained
Here, a novice is someone accepted into a Buddhist monastery in training before taking the full set of vows necessary to become a monk, i.e. before being ordained (made) a monk.

Seeing the Way
Buddhist Reflections on the Spiritual Life

13

An anthology of teachings by English-speaking disciples of Ajahn Chah

Christmas Humphrey
BUDDHISM
An introduction and guide

NAME: *Melissa*

WHAT I DO: *I have a normal life, really. I grew up in London, I live in a flat in London and have a very typical London lifestyle.*

MY FAMILY: *My grandmother's horrified that I'm a Buddhist. She thinks I've been brainwashed — however much I tell her that I haven't been! My father doesn't think there's anything sinister about it, but he's one of those people who just has no sense of religion. So to him it's a silly pursuit that doesn't lead anywhere. The rest of my family and my sisters are fine about it — one of my sisters is into spirituality in other ways.*

SOME OF MY SPECIAL INTERESTS: *I do have friends who aren't Buddhists and I go to the cinema a lot. But I suppose my heart-felt interests seem to be connected more and more with Buddhism.*

MY ROLE IN THE RELIGIOUS COMMUNITY

I'm quite involved with the Tibet Foundation, which sponsors education and activities promoting Tibetan culture. I also help run the Network of Buddhist Organizations, which is trying to enable Buddhist centres and organizations from all Buddhist traditions in Britain to come together for dialogue and joint activities.

My own connection is mainly via the Tibetan tradition of Buddhism. This developed when I was in India for nine months. I spent a while at a Tibetan monastery in Nepal. I went to Bodh-Gaya, the place of the Buddha's enlightenment, where there were lots of teachings and retreats going on. Then I went to Daramsala, seat of the Dalai Lama, where many Tibetan Buddhists are living in exile. I went in March, when the Dalai Lama gives teachings, and stayed for a three-month meditation retreat.

I first went to a Theravada Buddhist monastery – the one at Chithurst in Sussex – about three or four years ago. That was for a weekend. I really loved it. It just felt completely normal to me, being there.

FACT-FINDER

Retreat
Going on a retreat means going somewhere away from the distractions of everyday life in order to meditate or reflect.

Dalai Lama
Spiritual and political leader of the Tibetan Buddhists. Each new Dalai Lama is regarded as a reincarnation of the previous Dalai Lama.

WHERE I BELONG

I don't know where I belong. I don't know if I see myself belonging anywhere. I like to think I'm open-minded, that I can walk into any situation. I don't see myself fixed in one place or to one belief.

I do see myself as a Buddhist, so in a way I suppose you could say that I belong in the Buddhist community. Certainly, I've been coming here to Amaravati for as long as I can remember. I see it as a second home, I really do. It's like a home environment as well as a worshipping environment. It's not just like a church. We come here on camps and things. Mum started up a family camp which happens every summer with about a hundred people.

I get a real sense of community from Amaravati. It's like a family, and I think it's that which means the most to me. All around there's the metta, the loving-kindness, and you get a feeling from that. So I suppose I can see myself belonging here, but I don't really like the word 'belong'.

TISSA F

I feel I belong very much to this community at Amaravati. I feel I belong in a very real way, having actually been in the robe for a time. I've given a great part of my life to the Buddhist movement in one way or another – spare time when I was employed and much more time since retirement. It's a very central thing in my life.

MAURICE

FACT-FINDER

In the robe
In the robe of a Buddhist monk. (See pages 12–13.)

15

I don't belong anywhere. I think that probably comes from the fact that I was taken away from my birthplace against my will when I was sixteen. We lived in Lancashire but my parents wanted to move. After the move, I felt bereft. I grieved for the loss of my birthplace. I never ever found another place to call my own.

What I did find was a comfort in feeling that I belong in quietness and stillness, wherever I am and whatever I'm doing. I'm at home, if you like, with the emptiness, with the infinite. That sounds very religious, but it's how it feels for me. There's no place any more that I'm attached to.

MEDHINA F

Let's start at a material level. I was born in Australia, but I don't have any great sense of being an Aussie. When I do go back and visit my home country, though, I get a certain feeling of: 'This is the earth I'm made of.' I feel quite comfortable with travelling. Anywhere I go I feel comfortable.

In a spiritual sense, the question 'Where do I belong?' is really quite pertinent, quite relevant to me as a Buddhist. Buddhists talk about having no home, of not belonging anywhere, really. In our tradition, the aim and the fruit of our practice is to find contentment and comfort in the moment, wherever we find ourselves. To develop the ability to be at ease and at peace in any circumstances, pleasant or otherwise.

JITINDRIYA

For a Buddhist, the question of where I belong is a tricky one. It points to the very nature of self, and a main part of the Buddha's teaching is on this subject. He approaches it on two levels: the ultimate level and the conventional level. On the ultimate level, a Buddhist would say, 'I don't belong anywhere.' By identifying with the ego in ourselves – that is, by making ourselves individual and calling that individuality 'I' – we put a barrier up between ourselves and other people, the universe and the divine.

The Buddha's teaching identifies this sense of 'I' as a major problem. But there are practical ways of tackling it. We can live in a moral way. We can train our minds so that we can see into the ego, see through it and let go of self-centred concern. While we're on this path, we need some sort of protection. That's why, on a conventional level, a Buddhist would say that we place our sense of belonging in the Three Refuges. The Three Refuges are Buddha, Dhamma (the Buddha's teachings) and Sangha (the spiritual community of Buddhist nuns, monks, lay women and lay men). Or they can be recognized as wisdom, truth and virtue.

So in terms of belonging, if there's a 'me' and if I belong anywhere, I belong within the Three Refuges.

AMARO

FACT-FINDER

Lay
Here, not a (Buddhist) nun or monk.

Buddhism has given me a sense of all
people being equal. Race, colour, religion,
place – these things don't matter. They shouldn't
be a basis for division. So my affiliation to country
is fairly flimsy. When I'm abroad I'm British – that's
what's on my passport – but it's an identity for practical
purposes, really.

So I don't feel that I belong anywhere geographically.
If I belong in any place, it's in the heart of my teacher.
Wherever I am, whatever I'm doing, in my mind I try to
recollect the example of my teacher. That's my aim.
My teacher, His Holiness the Dalai Lama, embodies all that's
good and all that I could aspire to. If I keep his example close to
my heart, I have a feeling of being cared for and looked after and
nourished by my relationship with him. One isn't often in the physical
presence of one's teacher. It's through prayer and spiritual practice that
those feelings of being nurtured and cared for come.

MELISSA

FACT-FINDER

Dalai Lama
Spiritual and political leader of the Tibetan
Buddhists. Each new Dalai Lama is regarded
as a reincarnation of the previous Dalai Lama.

WHAT I FEEL STRONGLY ABOUT

I guess, in the deepest sense, what brought me into this life as a Buddhist nun are my strong feelings about human suffering. It doesn't seem necessary that we suffer so much. We create so much suffering just by not knowing each other, not knowing ourselves, not knowing our own minds. We create suffering by confusion and greed. Not always greed to feel guilty about but greed that comes from not knowing the powers at work within us as human beings. We create suffering not jus on a personal level but at a universal level – suffering through wars or difficult politics, for example.

The First Noble Truth is dukkha, and the Buddha's first teaching was about this. 'Dukkha' is translated as 'suffering', but it means much more than physical or mental pain. Dukkha is the whole sense of discontentment or inadequacy that come from being born into the world as a separate being. That is, having to be separated from love, having to die, having the pleasant as well as the unpleasant experiences being alive.

The Buddha said, 'I teach only two things: dukkha and the end of dukkha.' So the first thing we have to face up to is the fact that there is suffering. It's what most of u are trying to avoid. We don't like accepting responsibility for suffering. But when you begin to face up to the fact of suffering, you begin to understand its causes.

The cause of suffering, the Buddha said, is desire, grasping at what we think will be pleasant and save us from having to suffer. The end of suffering is letting go of that desire. To get to that point, we have to understand how the mind creates desire, why it does and what the objects of desire are. Once we understand that process, we can let go of desire. The Buddha suggested a way of getting there called the Eightfold Path. It's a path based on moral living and developing the mind. By developing the mind – our concentration, awareness, self-awareness – we develop our understanding. With our understanding we develop wisdom and with our wisdom we see clearly the way to be free of suffering.

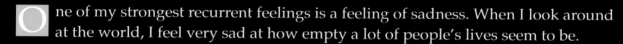

It's hard! That's why, when Buddhist monks and nuns are ordained, we say, 'I am fully committed to realizing this path.' That's why, at that point, we give up so much, because there's no point in trying to do it half-heartedly. But it's possible.

JITINDRIYA

One of my strongest recurrent feelings is a feeling of sadness. When I look around at the world, I feel very sad at how empty a lot of people's lives seem to be.

I believe that everything in the universe has its own nature, including human life and the human spirit. Human nature is sacred. I feel sad that I've been brought up, like most people, in ways that abuse it. Unwittingly, I've abused my own nature. I've abused the nature of others, people I love. I feel very sad about some of the things I did when I wasn't sufficiently aware not to do them. I feel sad about some of the things that have been done to me, out of the same ignorance in other people. One of my strongest feelings is: 'Isn't it a shame that everyone can't see things the way I see them.'

That's a feeling I have to work with. I'm not saying it's the right thing to feel, but at the moment it's how I do feel.

RON

I feel strongly that people have to work together. We're not islands. If we withdraw ourselves, become isolated and just live for our own pleasure, then things are going to collapse – things like the world, coherence, goodness. I think it's our responsibility, because we're alive and exist physically and have the ability to do something, to do something together. I think community is very important. So, in the same way, is family. Being with other people and working with other people is essential.

In Buddhism, there's the Sangha, the community of wise beings. The Buddha called it a Fourfold Sangha, made up of the community of ordained men, the community of ordained women, the community of lay men and the community of lay women. It's like the four legs of a table – four interdependent parts that together create the Sangha.

That interdependence of ordained people and lay people is one of the things that attracts me to the Theravada style of Buddhism. The Buddha set up the Sangha so that no part of it could become self-sufficient. To put it on a basic level, we have to come to the monastery here at Amaravati to feed the monks and nuns. This means we have regular opportunities to get spiritual help from them. The monks and nuns need to mix with lay people to be fed, and this lets them see what we need and what's happening in the world. It's a relationship which keeps the ordained people in touch with the world and helps us lay people look beyond it.

FACT-FINDER

Ordained/Lay people
Here, Buddhists who are/are not monks or nuns.

There are lay organizations of Buddhists in Britain, some of which are fine, some of which are less good. But I personally feel strongly that a sangha, a monastic organization, is the backbone to serious Buddhism. People have said, 'But you can't transplant this sort of thing to the West.' I think we've shown rather successfully that we can.

In Britain, there are not just sanghas of the Theravada school of Buddhism, to which I and Amaravati belong, but genuine, serious and good teachers of Tibetan Buddhism too. In fact, next week I'm going for the first time to a Tibetan centre in Scotland. There's Zen Buddhism in Britain as well, now. A lot of so-called Zen was pretty dodgy over here when people first started practising it, a few years ago. Now there are good Japanese-trained, Western teachers of Zen in this country.

Tibetan Buddhism is a bit too complicated for my taste, but I've learned enough about it to respect it. I was also attracted to Zen at one time. I visited Japan and stayed in Zen monasteries. The main claim of Theravada Buddhism is that it represents the original teaching of the Buddha, and what appeals to me about it is its simplicity. For instance, the monks and nuns, whatever their status, wear the same robes. Even the Patriarch wears exactly the same robes. But in Zen, which seems to be so simple, the roshis and the top people wear beautiful robes of scarlet, and of gold on some occasions. I must admit, I was quite surprised when I first saw this. I wasn't expecting it.

MAURICE

FACT-FINDER

Lay
Here, not including monks or nuns.

Monastic
Here, including monks and nuns.

Zen
This form of Buddhism developed in China and Japan.

Patriarch
Here, title given to the overall head of the Buddhist community in any Buddhist country. Similar in importance to 'Archbishop' in the Christian Church.

Roshi
Title meaning 'Master' given to someone authorized to teach Zen.

I feel strongly about human beings' arrogance with the world, about our inhumanity to each other and to other creatures. I'm very concerned about the rise of racist crime both in this country and elsewhere, about human-rights violations, about what the Chinese are doing to Tibet, about the tales of genocide and torture coming out of Bosnia, about the way live farm animals are transported long distances around Europe.

I feel overwhelmed by it. I do feel overwhelmed most of the time. I get very upset and despondent at the way things are. Then I wonder whether I shouldn't be doing more – things that are more socially engaged than networking Buddhist organizations, for instance, which is what I'm currently working on. I start thinking about whether I shouldn't be getting more involved politically, becoming more active that way. But then I question what politics can do when there's so much ignorance and hatred and intolerance of one another in the world.

Often, I get back to thinking that it's only through spiritual practice that you can really change things. Change has to happen in people's minds before we're going to see any real change in the world. But trying to hang on to that isn't easy. It's a real conflict for me.

MELISSA

W hat I feel strongly about depends on where I am – you never get a straight answer from a Buddhist! A strong focus of Buddhism is learning to be with reality as you find it. Suppose, for example, you're sitting in front of me with tears streaming down your face saying, 'I can't do anything right. My parents are blaming me for all their problems. I can't do anything to please them. What should I do?' At the time, this is the most important thing in the world to me. I'm not thinking about Bosnia, or Rwanda, or my own mother losing her eyesight. I'm thinking of you.

Obviously, Buddhists are concerned about the human world. We're concerned about the environment and bringing warfare to an end and increasing understanding in the world. But the only way we can do this is through our commitment to where we are and to who we're with. What matters is encompassing the needs of the moment and letting nothing go undervalued.

FACT–FINDER

Bosnia • Rwanda
Countries both torn by civil war when Amaro was speaking.

Novice
Here, someone accepted into a Buddhist monastery in training before taking the full set of vows necessary to become a monk or nun.

Ordained into a Buddhist monastery
Became a Buddhist monk/nun.

I could be talking to five hundred people at a conference or to half a dozen children at a primary school or to one of the novices here over the washing-up. Sometimes things that are said or events that occur can be particularly powerful, but you're not setting out to manufacture them. If you're used to being with the here-and-now, giving your heart to what you're doing, when the moment is right then you say and do the right thing. It comes out of the quality of honesty and commitment you're giving to the people you're with.

You don't find many do-gooders in Buddhism. Interest from Westerners in Buddhism tends to be as a way of contemplation and self-development. Nevertheless, freeing our own hearts from greed and selfishness, delusion and anger has an effect which ripples out to our children, to our friends, to the world around us, even if we never talk to anyone. I know of one person who ordained into a Buddhist monastery simply after seeing a Buddhist monk walking along a road in the early morning. She was so struck by the sight of him that she realized: 'I don't care what it takes, that's what I want to do. That's how I want to be.'

AMARO

I feel strongly about my religion. I can't say that I wouldn't consider anything else, that I'm going to spend the rest of my life as a Buddhist. But at the moment I can't really see myself going into another religion that's totally different.

I particularly like the Buddha's teachings about life and morality. They're down to earth, easy to grasp and easy to accept. He never used the word 'should'. It's up to you if you want to follow his guidelines.

I've learnt about the Dhamma, the Buddha's teachings, partly through Mum and partly through coming here, talking to the monks and nuns. At the summer camps that Mum set up, we have Dhamma lessons.

At school, some people think my being a Buddhist is all a bit weird. Most of them accept it, though for some it's more in the sense of 'better leave her to it'. I think it makes those people feel uncomfortable. Everyone on the RE course I do is strongly Christian, for instance. In fact, the course is mostly Christian based. We had a discussion once about life after death, but it was mainly about heaven and hell. Someone said, 'People who don't believe in God and don't repent go to hell.' I know who that was aimed at!

One friend I've had since my first year at secondary school now comes here to Amaravati. She comes on the summer camps as well. She was fairly wary towards Buddhism to start with. But once we'd broken through that barrier, she found it wasn't what she'd thought it was at all. She's really found that she likes the Buddhist way. A lot of people are more accepting than you expect, but there'll always be some that can't handle what they think of as 'weird'.

TISSA F.

FACT-FINDER

Don't repent
Here, aren't sorry because they have sinned, i.e. done wrong, broken God's laws.

MY FAVOURITE FESTIVAL

F estivals are important. Probably Vaisakha Puja, on the full moon of May, is the most important. According to our scriptures, the birth, the death and the enlightenment of the Buddha all happened on the full moon of May, so we celebrate these events on the same day.

We invite a lot of people to the monastery – it's a big festival day for the lay people. We usually have a big Dhamma offering and a food offering. It's like having lots of friends over for a party, everyone bringing something to eat. We have lunch together, then the Abbot or the Senior Monk gives a Dhamma talk to the people. We meditate together and usually do a circum-ambulation of the stupa. Then, as it gets dark, we light candles and do a meditation vigil.

Originally, stupas were burial mounds of a saint or a holy sage. Sometimes you'll still find relics in stupas. Generally, though, stupas are places that remind you of your aim towards a religious life. When we circumambulate – walk round – the stupa, which we do three times, it's to recollect the Holy Triple Gem. That's the Buddha, the Dhamma and the Sangha.

JITINDRIYA

FACT-FINDER

Vaisakha Puja
Also called Wesak, the name of the Buddhist (lunar) month in which this festival takes place. Some Buddhists, e.g. Zen Buddhists, celebrate only the birth of the Buddha at Wesak.

Our scriptures
Jitindriya means the three collections of Theravada Buddhist sacred texts making up the Tripitaka, which is thirteen times as long as the Bible.

Lay people
Here, Buddhists who are not monks or nuns.

Dhamma offering
Usually, a talk on the Dhamma, the teachings of the Buddha. Theravada Buddhists are encouraged to draw on their own experiences to illustrate and bring to life the meaning.

Vigil
Watch through the night.

Relics
Part of the bodies, clothing or possessions of holy people.

Holy Triple Gem
Also called the Three Jewels or Triple Refuge. (See also page 43.)

Sangha
Here, the whole community of Buddhists: monks, nuns and lay people.

25

I'm not really into big festivals. I prefer it when it's quiet. But, of the big festivals like Vaisakha, Kathina and Magha Puja, my favourite is Magha Puja.

Magha Puja hasn't really caught on much with lay people in the West yet. What happens here at Amaravati is that on the first day of Magha Puja all the bhikkhus, the ordained people, from the Theravada Buddhist monasteries in Devon, Northumberland and Sussex gather to see Luang Por, who is our head in England. It's as if a whole family's come together.

A few lay people are now realizing that this is a meeting they could be involved in, too. This year, invitations were sent out to the lay community, and on the second day of Magha Puja, we had a meeting of lay people and paid our respects to our teachers. About a hundred lay people attended. There was an offering of food and a puja service. Then Luang Por gave a talk. By sharing the day with him, we were able to show our respect to the Buddha, Dhamma and Sangha.

Officially, Magha Puja is a vigil on the night of the full moon, so there isn't really a second day. Often, though, you can't fit all the things you want to do at a festival into twenty-four hours. When you're fetching people from all over the country, and when you're trying to arrange a big meeting of lay people and ordained people, you just can't do it all in one day. At Amaravati, people start arriving for Magha Puja a couple of days in advance. The festival kind of grows according to the size and needs of the community.

MEDHINA F

FACT-FINDER

Vaisakha
Also called Wesak. (See also page 25.)

Kathina • Sangha
Kathina celebrates the Sangha, the whole community of Buddhists: monks, nuns and lay people. Offerings are made of cloth in the form of robes, one of the Four Requisites of Buddhist monks or nuns. (See page 9.)

Lay people
Here, Buddhists who are not monks or nuns.

Bhikkhus • Ordained people
Strictly, a bhikkhu is a Buddhist monk. Here, Medhina means all the monks and nuns.

Luang Por
Affectionate Thai title for a teacher. Here, Luang Por is Ajahn Sumedho, abbot of Amaravati.

Puja service
Ceremonial chanting by the whole community, with offerings of candles, flowers and incense on the main shrine.

Dhamma
The teachings of the Buddha. (See also page 43.)

Vigil
Watch through the night.

I suppose Magha Puja is the festival with the most festivities, when all the flags and things go up. It's in February. The date changes because it depends on the lunar calendar. Personally, I prefer Full Moon Time.

At Full Moon Time, people come to Amaravati and sit all the way through the night in meditation. I'm afraid I don't make it through the night, just a couple of hours at the most. But I think I prefer that sort of thing – less festivity, more appreciation.

We have Full Moon Time every month, or at least every lunar month. When we had a full moon last Thursday, Mum went and joined an all-night sit, but it's not possible for me if it's a school day.

We don't celebrate any of the Buddhist festivals at home. We tend to come here, to Amaravati. What we do celebrate at home is Christmas. Well, we don't celebrate it as a religious festival. Instead, we use it as a time to show our love and appreciation for friends and relatives by giving them presents. We don't have decorations around the house or a Christmas tree or anything like that. We just give presents, and cards maybe – though not Christmas cards.

TISSA F

FACT-FINDER

Magha Puja
See opposite.

Lunar calendar
Each month in this lunar calendar begins when there is a full moon and lasts only twenty-eight or twenty-nine days.

I used to live two or three hundred miles away from the nearest Buddhist monastery, so I've had very little experience of Buddhist festivals. But I have been involved in several Buddhist ceremonies. The most significant one for me was my ordination as a novice into the sangha here at Amaravati.

It was a pretty special event, partly because three of us ordained together – three is an auspicious number in Buddhism – and partly because all three of us were fairly mature spiritually. I think that special feeling came across to everyone there, to the sangha and to the lay supporters. I felt this tremendous goodwill from the lay people I'd formerly been part of. We'd supported the monks and nuns through their winter retreat and formed a close relationship. I felt I was being given a fantastic send-off by them and a fantastic welcome by the sangha.

There's some degree of ritual about shaving your head and taking off your lay clothes and putting on the white robes of the novice. But it's the ordination ceremony itself that leaves a lasting impression. At the ceremony, the novice receives the Eight Precepts, and this involves chanting them. Often the ceremony falls on an observance day, when the whole of the sangha receives the Eight Precepts. Then the novice chants them along with the rest of the sangha. But this wasn't an observance day. The three of us took the Precepts alone whilst the sangha chanted blessings in Pali: a line of monks on one side and nuns on the other. It was a wonderful feeling being at the centre of so much goodwill.

FACT-FINDER

Novice
Here, someone accepted into a Buddhist monastery in training before taking the full set of vows necessary to become a monk.

Sangha
Here, the community of monks and nuns at Amaravati. This term is also used to mean the wider Buddhist community of monks, nuns and sometimes lay people as well.

Auspicious
Favourable, significant, associated with blessings.

Lay people
Here, Buddhists who are not monks or nuns.

Pali
Ancient Indian language in which the main Theravada Buddhist sacred books are written.

Four Requisites
These are alms food, (monk's) robes, medicine (if needed) and shelter for one night. (See also page 9.)

The Eight Precepts are to refrain from harming any living being, from taking that which is not given, from erotic behaviour, from wrong speech, from using drink or drugs, from singing, dancing or entertainment, from eating at wrong times, and from lying on a high or luxurious sleeping-place. The first five are also available to lay people, although the precept about erotic behaviour is changed to restraint from things like adultery. The last three precepts are called the Renunciant Precepts. They're not about moral matters, they're restraints that you willingly take on as part of your further commitment to the holy life. Eating at wrong times means eating after midday.

Fully ordained monks have two hundred and twenty-seven rules they have to keep. Not breaking them requires a higher degree of mindfulness.

RON

I don't know whether I've got a favourite festival, but the one that I, like most Buddhists, try to keep in some way is Vaisakha. We get a lot of people coming to Amaravati then.

An important time for the monks and nuns is the Rains Retreat. In the East, this is between July and October, roughly, which is when the monsoon comes in India. It's wet and it's difficult to get about, so traditionally during the rains Buddhist monks and nuns would stay in one place, spending the time meditating and studying.

Here in the West, in spite of the different climate, the Rains Retreat is observed. It's still the period when ordinations take place – I was ordained at the beginning of this three-month retreat, for instance. The monks and nuns continue to observe the basic restrictions, like only going out on urgent business. But in England, mid- to late summer is also the time when most lay people want to come to the monastery: there are summer schools and things like that. So the monks and nuns have their much stricter retreat in the winter, during January and February, which in England is more sensible. Then they stop going out altogether and really get together and meditate and practise.

MAURICE

FACT-FINDER

Vaisakha
Also called Wesak. (See also page 25.)

Retreat
Going on a retreat means going somewhere away from the distractions of everyday life in order to meditate or reflect.

Ordinations
Here, ceremonies at which people become (Buddhist) monks or nuns. (See opposite.)

This is a difficult question for me to answer, because I'm living in Britain.

I've been to parts of India where there's a sizeable Buddhist population, and festival times there are very special. I was at Bodh-Gaya at the full moon in January and it was just amazing. There's a huge stupa near the bodhi-tree where the Buddha sat and reached enlightenment. People put thousands and thousands of little offering lamps, like night-lights, in great tiers around it and around the other stupas there. The place is just ablaze with little flames. The energy is intense. You really have a sense of something happening, a feeling of celebration.

In Britain, you get some of that by celebrating with a Buddhist community like Amaravati. That feeling of coming together and celebrating on auspicious days is important. If you do a particular practice or particular amount of practice on an auspicious day, it's said to have a more forceful and powerful energy from which there will be results. For example, the Dalai Lama is coming to Spain to give a teaching later this year, and it has to happen at the full moon.

MELISSA

FACT-FINDER

Stupa
Type of Buddhist shrine or sacred building.
(See also page 25.)

Auspicious days
Favourable or special days in the calendar associated with good luck and blessings.

Dalai Lama
Spiritual and political leader of the Tibetan Buddhists. Each new Dalai Lama is regarded as a reincarnation of the previous Dalai Lama.

A SPECIAL MOMENT

T he summer camps at Amaravati are special. You have to apply to get on them because so many people want places. The summer camp before last was really special for some reason. All our friends went on it – we make lots of friends on the summer camps. The Dhamma lessons were really good. I found them really significant. They meant something to me and I really appreciated them.

We worked on a water-garden for Amaravati. It's over there. We got it done in one week, which was quite amazing – real teamwork. Amaravati used to be a school, and we made the water-garden out of its old outdoor swimming-pool. The pool was derelict, with concrete and water-reeds all over the place. We lifted all the concrete slabs – a job in itself – and laid down gravel instead. We pulled up all the reeds and put in water-lilies. Working on it was a real bonding experience. It gave us a real feeling of community. That's one of the reasons why the summer camps are so special.

We could go to somewhere like Majorca in the summer, but I think this is better. There's more quality in it. I'm not saying there's anything wrong with Majorca. It's a good place for a holiday and relaxing in the sun. But at the end of one of the summer camps, you get a really good feeling from it. It's a feeling that stays with you.

TISSA F

FACT-FINDER

Dhamma
The teachings of the Buddha. (See also page 43.)

S ome people have these really amazing stories. They were somewhere when suddenly ... Significant things for me are not 'wham-bam' moments. For instance, just being near the Dalai Lama is significant.

Things tend to dawn on me slowly, so special moments are usually when with hindsight I see the significance of things – like small coincidences that add up. Perhaps we're being looked after in some way and led to the right places. At the time, it's not always easy to see.

MELISSA

FACT–FINDER

Dalai Lama
Spiritual and political leader of the Tibetan Buddhists. Each new Dalai Lama is regarded as a reincarnation of the previous Dalai Lama.

T here are a lot of special moments in a lifetime. Although this is going to seem negative, one special moment in my life as a Buddhist was my confirmation into the Church of England. I stood in front of the altar in a white dress making vows with this awful feeling in the pit of my stomach that I didn't know what I was talking about. It was a turning-point. I realized I was on the wrong path. I didn't reject God but I didn't know how to describe him or relate to him. I had to go and find out.

The first two years of finding out were spent amongst Christians. I went to different churches and spoke to different people. I would ask things like 'How can I believe in the Resurrection if there's no scientific evidence for it?' I firmly believed that eventually I would find the Christian God, but I kept coming to dead-ends. Then a teacher at my secondary school gave me a copy of a book called *Buddhism* by Christmas Humphreys. I recognized in Buddhism a way of understanding the Mystery.

FACT–FINDER

Confirmation into the Church of England
There are two stages in becoming a full member of the Church of England: baptism (often as a baby) and confirmation. At her confirmation, Medhina had to say publicly that she held Christian beliefs and promise to live a Christian life.

Resurrection
Rising of Jesus from the dead.

Christmas Humphreys (1901–1983)
A British lawyer, later a judge, who founded the Buddhist Society in London. He was an important figure in world Buddhism and summed up the common ground between the different schools (types) of Buddhism in his famous Twelve Principles of Buddhism.

In fact, through Buddhist teachings, I've been able to come to terms with Christianity, and now I feel comfortable with it. It's the Dhamma, the teaching of Buddhism, that helps make Christianity clearer to me. It's the Dhamma that brings me closer to the infinite. It helps me understand some of the questions that Christianity posed but didn't answer for me. It's my spiritual route.

MEDHINA F

The birth of my first baby, Cassandra Maria, was a tremendous change in my life. I'd wanted her for so long. I don't know anything that I'd wanted so much as having my own child. My middle name is Maria, which means 'longed-for child'. There's a tradition in my family that this is the name given to the first-born daughter. My mother's name is Maria. Her mother was Maria. I'd waited eight years for that baby.

When she was born, I was terrified at how dependent this little thing was on me. Suddenly, all the inspiration and love became tangled up with fear, the feeling of not being able to look after her. Also, up until then, I'd been involved in my career and my this and my that. So I felt total, abject despair at being superseded by another being who had complete rights over me. No matter how tired I was, no matter what I wanted, if that baby was hungry, tired or ill, if it needed me, I had no right to say no.

That was a big turning-point. I struggled hard against it. From somewhere deep down inside me, a voice was saying, 'What about me?' Then eventually it stopped. I'd given up part of my self to this new role. It was a big step to take.

Less than two years after that, the twins came along! But by then I was prepared. Three children under the age of two is a really hard training, but I do think it has made me what I am. It was really wonderful teaching. It was hard but it taught me a lot, gave me a lot of strength.

MEDHINA F

I think the special moment that comes to mind is when I first arrived in a Buddhist monastery in Thailand. From as early as the age of ten, I had a strong spiritual sense which I couldn't really express. Certainly it wasn't appropriate to try and voice it with the kinds of people I had as friends and family. Over the years, it developed into a sort of philosophy of life: life was good, harmlessness and kindness were good, peace and happiness were the heart of life but not easily attainable.

In the late 1960s and early 1970s, I was trying to apply that philosophy of goodness whilst at the same time having to cope with the traumas of teenage living. I was trying to please everybody, trying to be self-confident and uninhibited yet sensitive. I ended up feeling completely disorientated and alienated from other people.

By the time I'd reached my final year at university, I'd started drinking quite heavily. Even my friends, who were quite keen party-goers, were commenting on it. I was just drinking for oblivion really. I was beginning to doubt whether that sense of the spiritual and of truth and goodness I'd had all my life wasn't just a childish dream. I began to feel tremendous cynicism. The only reasonable response to life seemed to be despair and resentment. Eventually, I couldn't drink enough even to make a difference; the anguish would still be there. But in my heart I knew this wasn't a solution.

I resolved to do something. I was going to become a vegetarian. I was going to stop drinking. I was going on a spiritual journey to the East. Even so, the doubt was still there: 'A journey to the East? Come on, who are you kidding?' But I went – on a one-way ticket. I spent several months travelling, meeting various people en route. I came across interesting opportunities, but turned all of them down, until I came to a Buddhist monastery in North-East Thailand. From the start I really trusted the monks. They didn't want anything of me. There was no charge for staying at the monastery. I was welcome to stay for as long as I wanted. The only condition was that no-one could stay just as an observer. Everyone had to join in with the monastery routine. 'We don't take any passengers. You'll have to be crew!' they said. So I stayed for a while and, after a few weeks, joined as a novice.

Then I made the discovery which is my special moment. All through my life, I'd assumed there were only two ways of responding to any kind of desire. Either you followed it and got what you wanted, which pleased you for a while until you wanted something else. Or you didn't follow it and you felt frustrated. On my second day at the monastery, one of the novices told me that when a desire comes into your mind, you don't have to follow it. You don't have to push it away, either. You just watch it, then let it go. He said, 'Just recognize that a desire is the mind saying it wants something. Leave it at that. The desire will fade away.'

I thought, 'He's a novice, he doesn't know what he's talking about.' But I tried it in the next period of meditation we had. I'd seen a pineapple and wanted it. I felt hungry, and found that I could just observe the feeling. Sure enough, after a couple of minutes it had gone. To my amazement, the desire had gone but also the pineapple *wasn't missing*. Previously, desire had to be satisfied or you were left feeling empty. If you didn't want to feel empty you had to fill the space. But I didn't feel empty and the pineapple I'd wanted was still there. It just wasn't interesting any more. Life was complete, just as it was.

That convinced me I was following the right path. Part of the anguish and difficulty I'd been experiencing before was to do with not knowing how to deal with desire and fear. Now I understood I didn't have to make anything of it. I didn't have to identify with it, or claim it as mine, or fight it, or become obsessed with it. It was just a part of nature, like the wind in the trees. This was a significant moment, a revelation, and it led to my decision to become a Buddhist monk. My earlier cynicism and despair had been a false impression. That sense of the basic goodness of the world which I'd had since a child – that was the right instinct.

AMARO

FACT-FINDER

Novice
Here, someone accepted into a Buddhist monastery in training before taking the full set of vows necessary to become a monk.

The only unconventional thing I ever did up until a few years ago was to quit my job as an Environmental Health Officer. It was on the spur of the moment. People don't usually walk out of a job in local government, but I wasn't conscious of having any spiritual or religious motive for that, at least not at the time. I was just disillusioned with the work.

Then I had what you might term a conversion experience. It came as a total surprise. Until then, I'd never sensed anything at all that was mystical. All I knew was conventional reality, and I accepted that at face value. My conversion wasn't a gentle, pleasant experience, it was a sudden revelation. I was seeing things in a completely new way, with a different sort of consciousness to anything I'd ever known. Things that before had been confusing me fell into place. It was a very difficult experience to handle. It changed things forever.

Afterwards I wrote down what I'd experienced for a radio programme about faith which was looking at the subject of conversion experiences. I'll read you some bits. I've got the pages here:

'My whole body was trembling with the experience of being alive... I knew that at that moment I was alive forever. I was part of the infinite... I realized that I was living an eternity in those moments and that death therefore had no meaning or significance. My earthly body was a mere triviality...'

What's interesting is that, although I wasn't particularly aware of Buddhism at the time, so there would have been no conscious connection, what I describe fits the Buddhist view of life exactly.

Things were never really the same after that. It was a spark that started a change in me, not in any observable way initially. When I got married, my wife had had one big doubt. She said, 'You won't go off to be a monk or anything like that, will you?' With hindsight, that was a pretty intuitive concern. Last year, we split up. We both knew it was more a matter of when than if.

RON

For me, a special moment was when I decided that perhaps I really was a Buddhist. It was just after the War. I'd been through the War with no particular religious leanings. I did incline towards being a pacifist but decided that Hitler was just so bloody awful that I had to do something about it.

I'd read the Penguin book on Buddhism by Christmas Humphreys. It's still available now. I criticize it rather severely these days in some places, but it's extremely well written – a top lawyer making out a case for something he actually believed in! Having read his book, I began to feel, well, perhaps I've been a Buddhist all the time.

I remember walking up and down by the river at Richmond thinking, can I really accept that I'm a Buddhist? My thoughts turned on the idea of rebirth. Could I really believe that? I decided at the end of an hour or so that rebirth was at least highly probable. After that, I became a member of the Buddhist Society, and I've been involved with Buddhist activities ever since.

MAURICE

FACT-FINDER

Christmas Humpreys (1901–1983)
This British lawyer, later a judge, also founded the Buddhist Society in London. He was an important figure in world Buddhism and summed up the common ground between the different schools (types) of Buddhism in his famous Twelve Principles of Buddhism.

WORDS THAT MEAN A LOT TO ME

I like Buddhist chanting. It's quite powerful when you get all the monks and nuns chanting together, especially when it's a chant you're able to do as well. I've learnt a couple of chants. They're in Pali. For most of the time I've been coming here, the chanting has been in Pali, although some of the chanting is in English now. There's one chant in English which I particularly like. It's the Discourse on Loving Kindness chant and it describes loving-kindness.

Loving-kindness is 'metta' in Pali. The chant is quite a family favourite. You get the feeling of loving-kindness from the chant. It's nice to listen to it in Pali and let the chanting wash over you, but in English you hear the meaning, too. It's very meaningful. Mum knows it off by heart. She chanted it recently at my granddad's funeral.

TISSA F

FACT – FINDER

Pali
Ancient Indian language in which the main Theravada Buddhist sacred books are written.

I f I find myself in times of difficulty, I don't have a specific mantra or anything like that which I turn to. There is a tradition of mantras in Buddhism. You have your own personal word to help you. Personally, I find that I can be taken right out of everything else just by listening to a Dhamma talk or hearing a chant.

I'll do a chant for you if you like. This is the Discourse on Loving Kindness chant, which we used to do in Pali. Recently we translated it into English. I did it for my dad when he died.

Discourse on Loving Kindness

This is what should be done
By those who are skilled in goodness
And who know the path of peace:
Let them be able and upright,
Straightforward and gentle in speech,
Humble and not conceited,
Contented and easily satisfied,
Unburdened by duties
And frugal in their ways,
Peaceful and calm
And wise and skilful,
Not proud and demanding in nature;
Let them not do the slightest thing
That the wise would later reprove,
Wishing in gladness and in safety
That all beings may be at ease,
Whatever beings there may be
Whether weak or strong,
Omitting none –
The great and the mighty,
Medium, short or small,
The seen and the unseen,
Those living near and far away,
Those born and to be born –

May all beings be at ease;
Let none deceive another
Or despise any being in any state;
Let none through anger or ill-will
Wish harm upon another,
Even as a mother
Protects with her life
Her child, her only child,
So with a boundless heart
Should we cherish all living beings,
Radiating kindness
Over the entire world –
Upwards to the skies
And downwards to the depths,
Outward and unbounded.
Free from hatred and ill-will,
Whether walking or standing,
Seated or lying down,
Free from drowsiness,
One should sustain this recollection.
This is said to be
The sublime abiding:
By not holding too fixed a view,
Having clarity of vision,
The pure-hearted one,
Being free from all sense desires,
Is not born again into this world.

dukkha

anicca

anatta

There are three words from Buddhism that help me understand the world: 'dukkha', 'anicca' and 'anatta'.

Dukkha is unsatisfactoriness, and worldly things are ultimately unsatisfactory. So when things are starting to feel unsatisfactory, you just think, 'Yes, well, that's how the Buddha says they are.'

'Anicca' means that all things change. So if you're trying to come to terms with something that's gone, something you didn't want to go, well, all things change. Good things change. Bad things change.

'Anatta' means 'not-self'. The things we tend to think of as ourselves – our intelligence or our looks or our bodies or our thoughts – these are not part of our inner selves. So if you lose your looks or you find you're in pain, that's not self, that's something which is dukkha or anicca.

Dukkha, anicca and anatta put everything into perspective. They help me reflect on the world I live in and accept it. I don't cling on to things or want them always to be the same. I don't want life not to hurt. This is the way things are.

MEDHINA F

Communication is important. One of the reasons why people can't get on in the world is that we can't communicate very well. We don't listen. We misunderstand each other. It's a source of many problems. For me, the words I choose are important.

There are a lot of words in Buddhism that I come back to, words like 'peace', 'wisdom', 'liberation of the heart', 'freedom'.

'Freedom' is a very important word. When I was at art school in Australia, art was my life. I made so many discoveries that I didn't know why it wasn't compulsory for everyone to go to art school! I remember at that time coming across something that one of the great philosophers had said: 'The greatest freedom comes from the strictest discipline.' I understood it immediately. I already knew the problems people can create for themselves by following their desires. Our minds are too limited to cope with our desires, and following my desires had actually become my prison.

It's a wonderful paradox, isn't it, freedom and discipline? The Buddha saw that the way of freedom from suffering is to go through the suffering – to see what suffering is, to understand it, to restrain yourself from acting in any way that causes harm. Because any harm you cause is only an obstacle to your own peace of mind. It limits your ability to have insight into the nature of things and to free yourself from ignorance.

JITINDRIYA

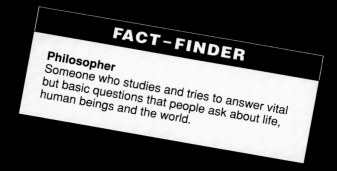

FACT-FINDER

Philosopher
Someone who studies and tries to answer vital but basic questions that people ask about life, human beings and the world.

Y ou might have noticed that I'm a wordy person! I'm very much at home in the world of words. There is a beauty and a power in being able to point to the nature of things with words – although obviously there are limits to what the human mind can think and describe.

I have a little notebook which was given to me in which I write down and keep quotable quotes. Maybe half of them are from the Buddhist tradition, the rest are from all over the place – Shelley, the Hindu Upanishads, Shakespeare, Sufi Muslim poets, James Joyce – the whole kaboodle. The Buddha pointed out that: 'Any wise words you hear, if you have faith in me, count them as having come from my mouth.' He's basically saying, 'Don't worry where the words come from, if they're meaningful to you and they work, use them.'

At the present time, the human realm of the world seems to be in a delicate balance. So the need to communicate a sense of the spiritual truth and make it accessible and meaningful to people is extremely important. Having insight and spiritual qualities yourself is one thing, communicating them is another. Communicating isn't just expressing these qualities or displaying them, it's offering them in a form that another person can receive, so that they can literally take them in and make use of them. There's no point in doing this if your purpose is just to create wonder or amazement.

So where words have their importance and power – even though they may just be words – is in pointing to things within us which we are capable of changing, to ways of enriching our lives.

AMARO

The word 'compassion' is important to me. I feel a bit embarrassed talking about it, because I realize I don't have any a lot of the time. But what's more important than the word is the aspiration, the aim, and compassion is something that I do aspire to. Compassion with wisdom. Compassion is the genuine sense of wanting to help others reduce their suffering. Wisdom is approaching that from a place where you can see the way things truly are.

Another word that's important to me is 'guru', teacher. The Buddha was a teacher, and serious Buddhists will try to seek out a teacher for themselves. The teacher–student relationship can lead to problems, and the Buddhist scriptures advise us to check out potential teachers very thoroughly. You're making a big commitment. Once you've found someone you trust, who you believe embodies the appropriate qualities, who is virtuous and worthy, there's a responsibility from both sides.

I believe that my teacher, His Holiness the Dalai Lama, embodies the wisdom and compassion of the Buddha. I'm extremely grateful to be one of his students. Sometimes I feel saddened that I can't be with him very often. But being a student isn't about traipsing around the world to hear teachings. It's what you do in order to transform your mind and develop the qualities you see exemplified by your teacher.

MELISSA

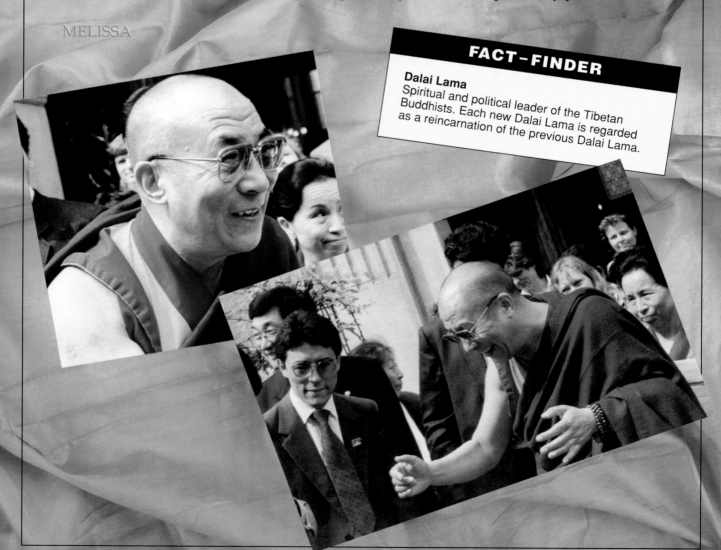

FACT-FINDER

Dalai Lama
Spiritual and political leader of the Tibetan Buddhists. Each new Dalai Lama is regarded as a reincarnation of the previous Dalai Lama.

Buddha–Dhamma–Sangha, the Triple Gem or the Triple Refuge, that's important and significant to me. There's a depth and range of meaning to each of the three parts of the Triple Gem.

Buddha is both the person who founded Buddhism and a quality of inner awareness. 'Buddha' means 'awakened one'. It's said that we all have a Buddha nature, a clear awareness of the nature of things. It's said that it's already awake in us, but in most people it's blocked and obscured. It's there, though, and you can take refuge in it.

Dhamma is both the teachings of the historical Buddha and also the truth. It's not the sort of truth that can be written down in books but the sort of truth you can only experience for yourself. It's the way things are. You can take refuge in the truth.

Sangha is the ordained community. You can broaden the definition to include lay Buddhists, and you can use the word to refer to a pure life. You can take refuge in a pure life.

RON

FACT-FINDER

Ordained community
The community of (Buddhist) monks and nuns.
Lay Buddhists
Those who are not monks or nuns.

THINGS I FIND CHALLENGING

L ife at Amaravati is challenging because you're living closely in a community of people that you wouldn't necessarily choose to live with. When you're under a vow of restraint, your emotions and desires are more likely to come to the surface and be frustrated. This is one of the reasons for living under restraint. When your desires and frustrations reach the surface, you can see them and contemplate them and understand how to let go of them. But when you're living together with other people who are going through the same process, there is the possibility for conflict. Also, we're a community of sixteen different nationalities, so there's quite a range of cultural conditioning and views on things.

It's a challenge and at the same time it's a great ground for insight. We share the same intention of understanding and giving up the negative emotions, of cultivating kindness, peace and patience, which makes community life very, very pleasant. You really notice it when you go outside and meet people who haven't had this kind of training – not that they're expected to. For instance, they seem to be shouting at each other, talking at the same time as each other, not really hearing what each other has to say. And this is called conversation!

In the community, we develop a sensitivity and an ability to listen, and not just to external things – meditation is listening to the mind and the heart. So community life does change you. I think friends who knew me before I became a nun would probably notice more about me that's changed than I do myself, though.

JITINDRIYA

FACT-FINDER

Vow of restraint
Ron talks on page 29 about some of the things that Buddhist monks and nuns promise not to do.

B uddhism is a challenge to me to look at myself. I think the essence of Buddhist training is getting wise to one's self, or one's non-self, if you like. You discover that, whatever you thought your self was, it isn't quite like that. Buddhism challenges you to examine your conscience, although I'm not very keen on that word. It challenges you to examine your thoughts, feelings, emotions. If you feel in an ugly mood, a Buddhist response would be to ask yourself, 'What's wrong? What's causing this?'

It's also a challenge to keep going with meditation and so on. The ultimate aim of meditation is to break through to a more profound realization of the true nature of things. But until you've got there, this is something which is inevitably going to be outside your experience, which you're bound to feel unsure about.

MAURICE

Save the Dolphins

O h, self-improvement is the challenge, definitely. I see my own faults writ large before me all the time, and the challenge is to work with my anger or my bad temper or my lethargy. Other people might say to me, 'But you're so patient,' or 'You're so busy.' Outsiders might see me as a really placid person. On the other hand, the girls see me at home. They know I lose my temper. They know I go mad at the state of the bedroom floor and things like that.

I need to get all of that into perspective. I'm not the world's best, nor the world's worst. The challenge is to get a true perspective on where I am, to work on my self and improve it.

MEDHINA F

45

We have a Pali word 'Atthangika- magga'. It refers to what we call in English the 'Eightfold Path'. 'Magga' in Pali means 'path'. Now, I'd always visualized that path as being a great big track. Then not so long ago someone pointed out to me that the word in Sanskrit which the Pali word 'magga' comes from doesn't actually mean a path in the sense of a road. It's more like the trail an animal leaves. It's a word that hunters would use when trailing an animal. Now here was a discovery. 'A trail,' I thought, 'That's more like the reality of it.'

We have to develop the eye of the hunter to follow the trail, not just to keep to the track but to see where it is. The thinking mind and the ego are intelligent and slippery customers. In most spiritual traditions and in the writings of contemplatives and mystics over the ages, what's said to be the most difficult thing is stopping the ego, the self-centred perspective within us, taking hold of our spiritual practice and organizing it, rationalizing it. This self-centredness is pretty good at wearing disguises. It can appear discerning or sensitive or wise. And it works subtly.

I'm still very young, really. This is one of the largest Buddhist centres in Britain and the biggest community of Buddhist monks and nuns in the Western world. I find myself regularly in charge of it. I'm increasingly in teaching roles and leadership roles. There are plenty of opportunities for getting it all out of balance, for losing sight of where the purpose is. People can also project their own needs onto you. They meet you thinking or wanting you to be a great cosmic spiritual master when what you are is Joe Normal.

So keeping a sense of where the path is in the midst of one's own tendencies towards self-concern and delusion and desire, that's where I find the challenge is. Keeping the recollection that it's the moment that matters. After all, we're not on the way to anywhere else. If the moment is open and clear, everything good flows from that, everything works.

We have two forces in us, and these are headed in opposite directions. There's the lazy, selfish tendency that wants to crawl back into the womb. It doesn't want to experience life because it's so much cosier to be oblivious to it. Opposed to this, there's aiming at enlightenment. The challenge is to have the courage to aim at enlightenment.

Part of the challenge is being patient. I have total faith that I'm following a good spiritual path. I'm also aware that it's not an easy path or a fast path. But sometimes I think it's possible to become preoccupied with distant goals. I should be concentrating on the present moment, even if it's painful or unsatisfactory. This is where the journey really happens.

RON

FACT-FINDER

Pali
Ancient Indian language in which the main
Theravada Buddhist sacred books are written.

Sanskrit
Ancient Indian language used in most Hindu
and some (Mahayana) Buddhist sacred books.

Eightfold Path
The Buddha taught that this way of living and
training the mind leads to the end of dukkha
(suffering). (See also page 18.)

INDEX

Page numbers in **bold** type show where words or phrases are explained in FACT-FINDERS